dabblelab

1O-MINUTE
ENGINEERING
PROJECTS

BY SARAH L. SCHUETTE

CAPSTONE PRESS
a capstone imprint

Dabble Lab is published by Capstone Press, an imprint of Capstone.
1710 Roe Crest Drive, North Mankato, Minnesota 56003
www.capstonepub.com

Editorial Credits
Editor: Shelly Lyons; Designer: Tracy McCabe;
Media Researcher: Tracy Cummins; Production Specialist: Katy LaVigne;
Project Production: Marcy Morin

Photo Credits
All photographs by Capstone: Karon Dubke

Design Elements
Shutterstock: ArtMari, best_vector, BewWanchai, Bimbim, Bjoern Wylezich, Dr Project, drpnncpptak, hchjjl, Kalinin Ilya, Shorena Tedliash-vili, Smiling Fox, Tukang Desain, unpict, Valentain Jevee

Library of Congress Cataloging-in-Publication Data is available on the Library of Congress website
ISBN 978-1-5435-9093-7 (library binding)
ISBN 978-1-5435-9099-9 (eBook PDF)

Summary: Searching for easy engineering projects for your makerspace? You've come to the right place! From winches and gears to bridges and marble runs, these 10-minute STEM projects will have kids making in no time!

All internet sites appearing in back matter were available and accurate when this book was sent to press.

Printed in the United States   4052

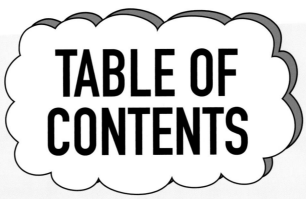

TABLE OF CONTENTS

GOT 10 MINUTES?

Grab some supplies and get started! These quick and easy engineering projects will inspire you. Simple supplies and easy directions will have you making in no time! Don't forget to clean up after yourself when you're done.

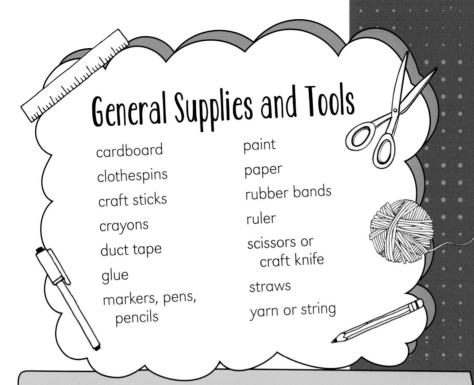

General Supplies and Tools

cardboard

clothespins

craft sticks

crayons

duct tape

glue

markers, pens, pencils

paint

paper

rubber bands

ruler

scissors or craft knife

straws

yarn or string

Tips

- Gather the supplies and tools needed before starting a project.

- Ask an adult to help you with sharp tools.

- Use a toolbox to hold your building supplies. You can build on the go and stay organized.

- Change things up! Don't be afraid to make these projects your own.

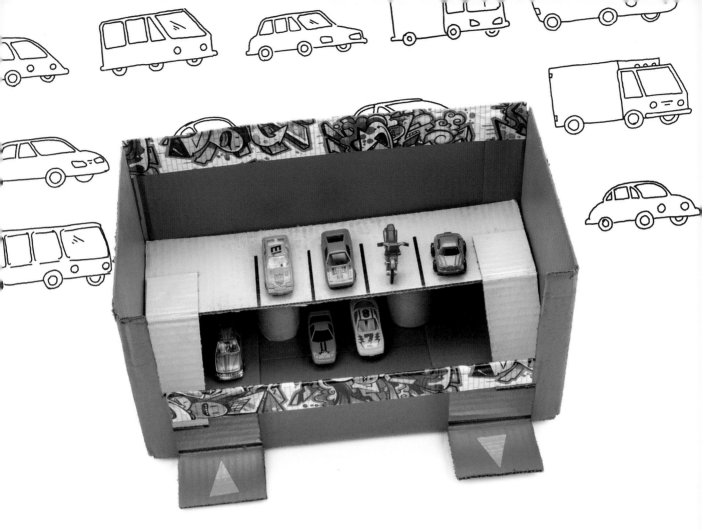

PARKING GARAGE

Engineers design and build things all around us.
You can think like an engineer too! Try designing
and building a parking garage.

What You Need:

cardboard box

scissors or craft knife

paper-towel tube

duct tape

pencils, pens, markers,
   paint, or crayons

What You Do:

1 Cut the flaps off a cardboard box.

2 Cut two holes in the front of the box to make an entrance and exit. Also cut off the top front of the box.

3 Cut two pieces, each 2.5 inches (6.4 centimeters) long, from a paper-towel tube. Set the pieces inside the box as support pillars.

4 Use the cardboard flaps to make ramps. Set them on top of the tube pieces. Duct tape the pieces together.

5 Decorate the garage with paint, markers, and duct tape.

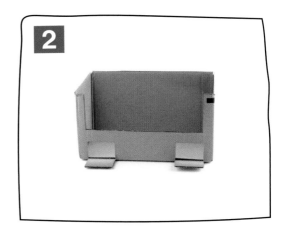

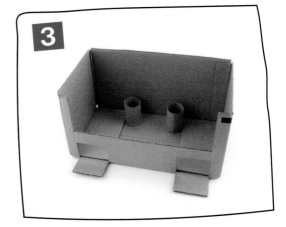

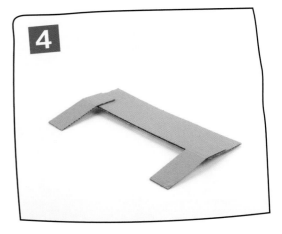

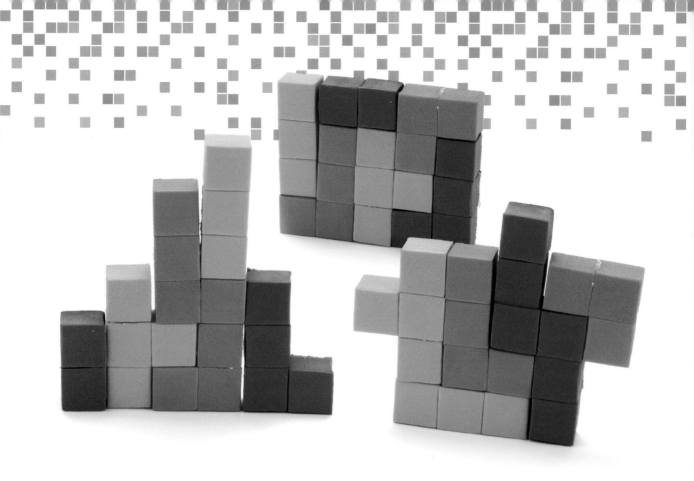

BUILDING BLOCK PUZZLE

Engineers often have to solve problems or puzzles
to help make a design work. Are you a puzzler?
Find out with these fun polyomino puzzles!

What You Need:

foam cubes (at least 20)

glue

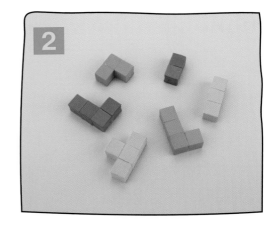

What You Do:

1 Sort the cubes into groups of 2, 3, and 4.

2 Glue the cubes together to make different shapes.

3 Place the cube shapes together like puzzle pieces. Create one large rectangle or another fun shape.

4 Take the puzzle apart and make new shapes.

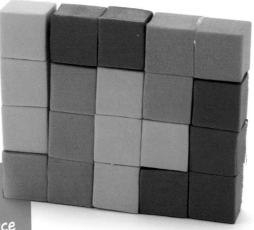

TIP Before gluing your foam cubes together, try rearranging them on a flat surface to create the puzzle you want. Once you know the shape, glue the cubes together.

JUMPING
JACK

Sometimes simple materials can be turned into
a useful device. Watch how paper cups, a dowel,
and straws become a fun machine!

What You Need:

- scissors
- paper
- straw
- glue or tape
- 2 paper cups or cardboard tubes
- hole punch
- dowel or craft stick
- pipe cleaner

What You Do:

1 Cut two identical people shapes out of paper. Cut a straw in half and glue or tape it between the two paper shapes.

2 Punch two holes across from each other in each cup. Slide one end of the dowel through one cup's holes.

3 Slide the straw with the paper shapes onto the dowel. Slide the remaining dowel end through the other cup's holes.

4 Bend a pipe cleaner in a loop and connect it to the dowel on each side of the paper shape.

5 Glue the other straw half to one end of the dowel to make a crank.

6 Turn the crank and watch Jack jump!

TIP If Jack moves with the jump rope, reposition the jump rope and make sure the paper shapes are balanced.

BRIDGE IT!

It can take a team of engineers years
to design and build a new bridge. But you
can build one in just 10 minutes!

What You Need:

6 pencils, 4 sharpened

6 rubber bands

cardboard, about 6x4 inches
   (15x10 centimeters)

tape or glue

8–10 craft sticks

What You Do:

1 Cross the eraser ends of two pencils to make a V. Wrap a rubber band around the ends.

2 Repeat step 1 with two other pencils. Then stand up each pencil V on a long end of the cardboard. Stick the sharpened end of each pencil into the cardboard to keep in place.

3 Tape or glue the craft sticks together to make a bridge deck. Tape two more pencils to the long edges, leaving each end sticking out past the sticks.

4 Place the bridge deck between the Vs. Wrap rubber bands where the pencils meet.

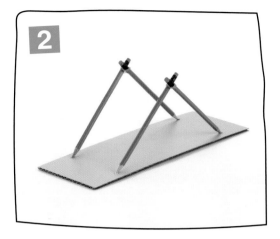

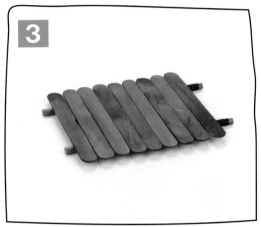

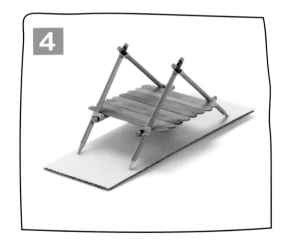

TIP Test it out! Try putting cars or building blocks on the bridge. How much weight can it hold? How could you redesign the bridge to make it stronger?

13

KICK BALL

Engineering isn't all about work! Simple machines like levers make work easier. Clothespins act as levers in this fun game. A twist of a dowel moves a lever, and the lever pushes the load (a ball).

What You Need:

scissors or craft knife

cardboard box, shoebox size

6 regular sized clothespins, two colors

hole punch

4 dowels

washi tape or markers

pom-pom

What You Do:

1 Cut a square out of each end of a box to make goals.

2 Clip two clothespins of one color to a dowel. Then clip one clothespin of the same color to the middle of another dowel. Repeat with the other color clothespins.

3 Set the dowels on the top edge of the box, spacing them evenly. From the bottom of the box, draw a 2 1/2-inch (6.4-cm) line up toward each dowel end. Then punch a hole at each line's end.

4 Slide the dowels into the holes. The clothespins should hang above the bottom of the box without touching it.

5 Decorate the bottom and sides of the box with tape or markers.

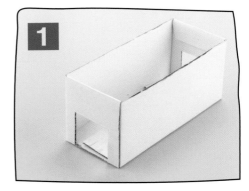

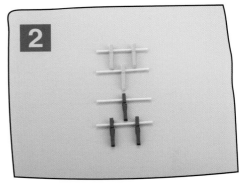

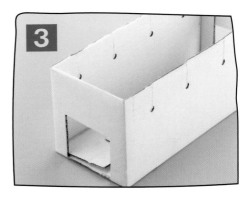

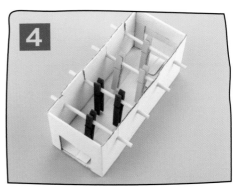

TIP When you're ready to play, add a pom-pom, twist the dowels, and watch the levers hit the pom-pom into a goal. Score!

15

ROOSTER RACER

Repurpose pool noodles! Build rooster racers with your friends and see which one reaches the finish line first.

What You Need:

scissors or craft knife

pool noodles

round toothpicks

straw

craft stick

glue or tape

What You Do:

1 Slice or cut pool noodles into rooster shapes.

2 Use four circles to make wheels. Stuff an extra piece of noodle into the center hole of each of the wheels. Stick a toothpick into the center of two wheels.

3 Cut two 1-inch (2.5-cm) pieces of straw. Slide one straw piece onto each toothpick. Stick the toothpicks into the other two wheels.

4 Glue or tape a craft stick to the straws. The piece will look like a skateboard with large wheels.

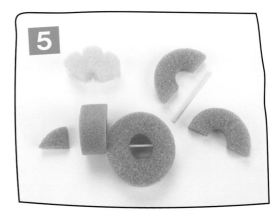

5 Connect different shapes and sizes of noodle slices with toothpicks to make a rooster. Glue it to the craft stick.

TIP You can connect and build anything with pool noodle slices and toothpicks. Try building a tower or bridge!

FLYING
FISH

If roosters can race, then fish can fly! Design your
own zip line and watch gravity at work. Get zipping!

What You Need:

marker
cardboard
scissors
2 paper clips
string
chairs
duct tape

What You Do:

1 Draw an outline of a fish about as big as your hand on cardboard. Cut it out.

2 Unbend the paper clips to make two S shapes.

3 Duct tape the paper clips to the fish, then cover the entire fish with tape as well.

4 Draw a funny face on your fish.

5 Bend the top of the paper clips outward.

6 Tie a string between two chairs of different heights. Hang the fish on the string at the high end. Push the fish and watch it fly!

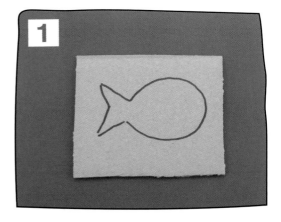

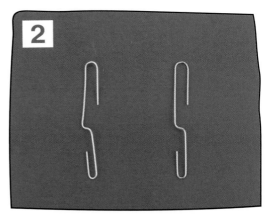

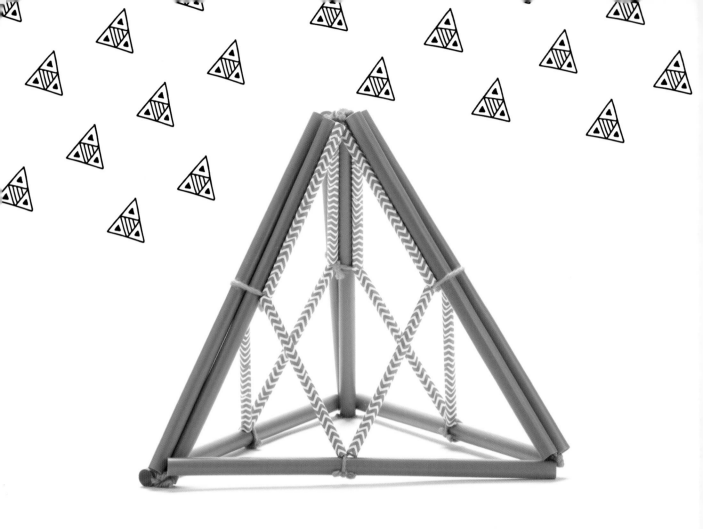

TRIANGLE CRAZE

Triangles are a common shape used in architecture.
They add stability and strength to a structure.
Experiment with this important shape
by building this pyramid of triangles!

What You Need:

15 straws

yarn

scissors

What You Do:

1 Thread yarn through three straws. Tie the ends of yarn together to make a triangle. Repeat to make two more triangles.

2 Cut two other straws in half. Thread yarn through the four pieces and tie the ends to make a diamond. Repeat to make two more diamonds.

3 Form a pyramid with the triangles. Tie a diamond to the top, sides, and bottom of the pyramid on each side.

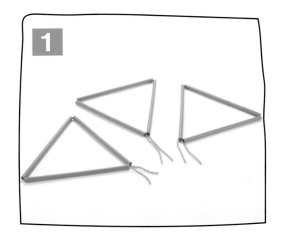

1

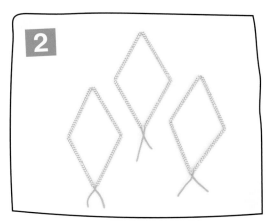

2

3

TIP Try working with friends to build a larger structure. Watch how high your pyramid stacks can get!

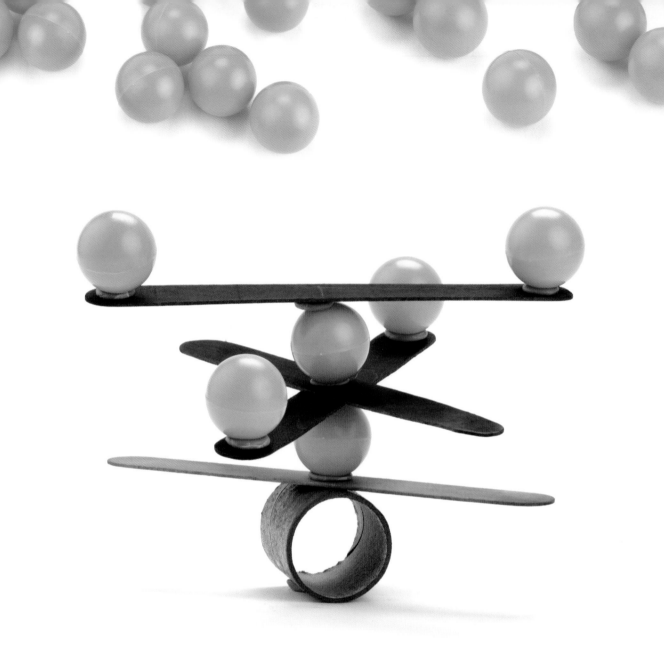

BALANCE IT!

Engineering meets modern art in this simple
sculpture. How high can you go? Can you balance it?

What You Need:

table tennis balls

large craft sticks

poster putty or clay

cardboard tube

What You Do:

1 Attach table tennis balls to craft sticks with putty.

2 Stack the sticks and balls on top of each other.

3 Add a cardboard tube beneath the bottom stick. Adjust the putty to make the sculpture balance.

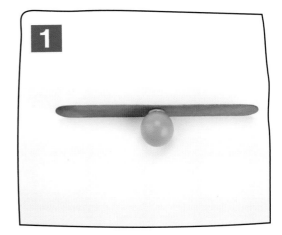

TIP For best results, make sure your working surface is flat. For an extra challenge, try adding more balls, sticks, and tubes to the structure.

ROLL IT UP!

Even engineers need to improve their designs to make sure buildings will not collapse. Test the strength of these simple paper tubes. How much weight can they hold before they collapse? Try it and find out!

What You Need:

6 pieces of paper

tape

different "loads" (books, toy cars, building blocks)

What You Do:

1 Roll each piece of paper into a tube. Tape along the long edge.

2 Stand the tubes together and place a notebook or two on top.

3 Set toys or building blocks on top of the notebooks.

TIP Try adding different loads on top of the notebooks. How much can the tubes hold before they crumple from the weight? For even more challenges, try changing the number of tubes. How many tubes are needed to hold one textbook?

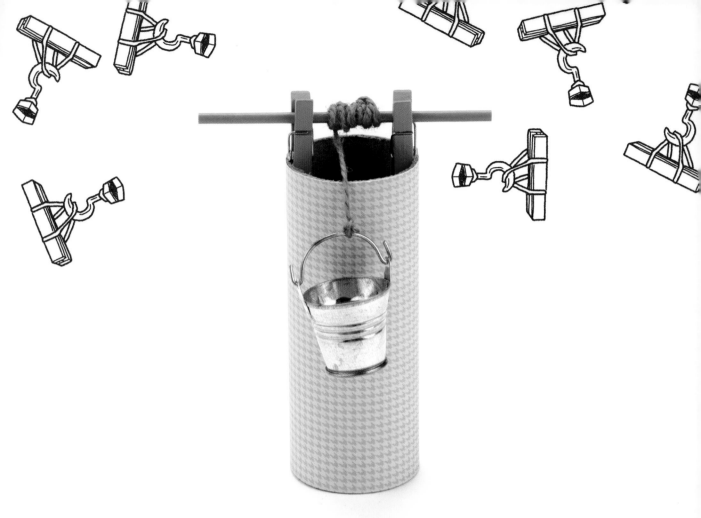

WINCH WAY?

Pulleys and winches are simple machines that make work easier. See for yourself. Winch way will it go?

What You Need:

cardboard tube

craft paper or washi tape

2 mini clothespins

string or yarn, about 8 inches (20 cm) long

lollipop stick

scissors

small bucket or cup with handle

What You Do:

1   Cover a cardboard tube with craft paper or washi tape.

2   Clip the clothespins to the stick. The stick should rest loosely in the holes of the clothespin.

3   Tie one end of the string to the center of the stick. Tie the other end to the handle of the bucket.

4   Glue the clothespins to the inside of one end of the cardboard tube.

5   Twist the stick to make the bucket go up and down.

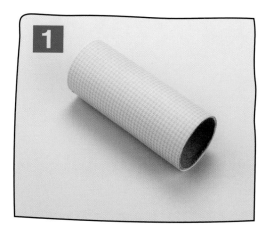

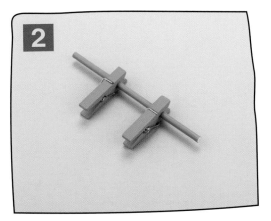

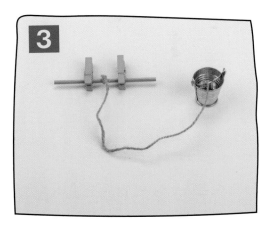

MARBLE
A-MAZE-ING

Make your next marble run portable!
It will be a-maze-ing!

What You Need:

cardboard lid or shallow box

craft sticks

wooden blocks

tape, washi tape, or glue

clear plastic place mat
  or sheet

scissors

marble

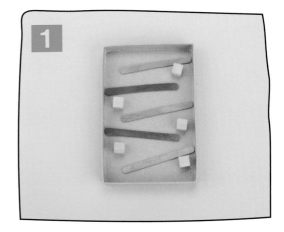

What You Do:

1 Set the craft sticks and wooden blocks in the lid. Plan where you want them to go. Tape them to the box to test your maze.

2 Once you have a design you like, glue the sticks and blocks to the lid.

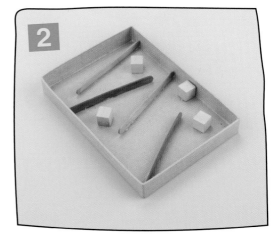

3 Put a marble in the maze. Lay the plastic on top of the lid and cut it to fit.

4 Tape the plastic piece to the lid. Decorate the sides with more tape.

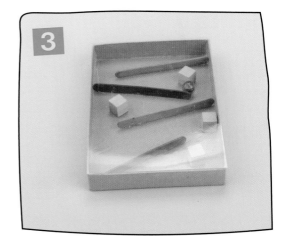

5 Move the box back and forth to try and get the marble through the maze.

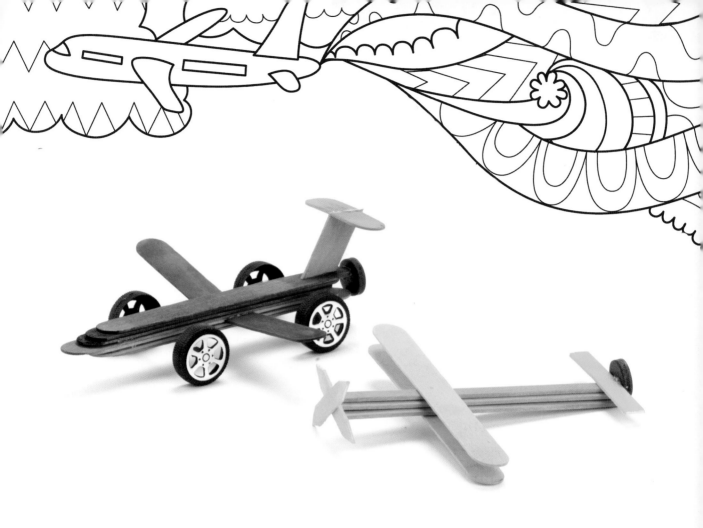

MAGNET PLANE

Combine wings, wheels, and a magnet to create a simple airplane. Use a bar magnet to watch your plane really move!

What You Need:

9 large craft sticks
hot glue gun or duct tape
plastic wheels or bottle caps
straw
2 toothpicks
scissors
craft magnet
bar magnet

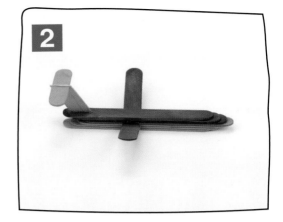

What You Do:

1 Stack seven craft sticks on top of each other to look like an airplane. Glue or tape them together.

2 Cut the remaining two craft sticks in half. Cut one of the sticks in half again. Glue the pieces to the plane to make wings and a tail.

3 Cut two small pieces of straw, shorter than the toothpicks. Slide the straws onto the toothpicks.

4 Connect a wheel to each end of the toothpicks. Glue the straw pieces to the bottom of the plane.

5 Glue a craft magnet to the back of the plane. Hold a bar magnet near the back of the plane to repel the craft magnet. Watch your plane move!

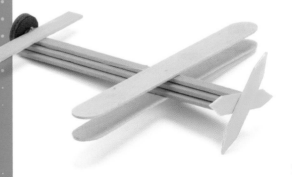

Read More

Enz, Tammy. *Engineering Projects to Build On: 4D An Augmented Reading Experience*. North Mankato, MN: Capstone Press, 2019.

Schwartz, Heather E. *Cool Engineering Activities for Girls*. North Mankato, MN: Capstone Press, 2012.

Westing, Jemma. *Out of the Box*. New York: DK Publishing, 2017.

Internet Sites/Resources

CuriOdyssey Science Playground and Zoo: Science Experiments for Kids: How to Make Hoopsters
https://curiodyssey.org/activities/science-experiments-for-kids/how-to-make-hoopsters/

Made for STEAM: Projects for Ages 9+
https://www.madeforsteam.com/9-and-up

Science Buddies: Bridge Building Bonanza: Which Design Wins?
https://www.sciencebuddies.org/stem-activities/bridge-building-designs